101 FACTS ABOUT
TROPICAL FISH

Please visit our web site at: www.garethstevens.com
For a free color catalog describing Gareth Stevens Publishing's list of high-quality books and multimedia programs, call 1-800-542-2595 (USA) or 1-800-387-3178 (Canada). Gareth Stevens Publishing's Fax: (414) 332-3567.

Library of Congress Cataloging-in-Publication Data

Williams, Sarah, 1976-
    101 facts about tropical fish / Sarah Williams. — North American ed.
      p. cm. — (101 facts about pets)
    Includes bibliographical references and index.
    ISBN 0-8368-2892-5 (lib. bdg.)
    1. Tropical fish—Miscellanea—Juvenile literature. 2. Tropical fish—Behavior—Miscellanea—Juvenile literature. [1. Tropical fish—Miscellanea. 2. Aquariums.] I. Title: One hundred one facts about tropical fish. II. Title. III. Series.
    SF457.25.W56   2001
    639.34—dc21   2001031055

This North American edition first published in 2001 by
Gareth Stevens Publishing
A World Almanac Education Group Company
330 West Olive Street, Suite 100
Milwaukee, WI 53212 USA

This U.S. edition © 2001 by Gareth Stevens, Inc. Original edition © 2001 by Ringpress Books Limited. First published by Ringpress Books Limited, P.O. Box 8, Lydney, Gloucestershire, GL15 4YN, United Kingdom. Additional end matter © 2001 by Gareth Stevens, Inc.

Ringpress Series Editor: Claire Horton-Bussey
Ringpress Designer: Sara Howell
Gareth Stevens Editor: Heidi Sjostrom

Printed in Hong Kong through Printworks Int. Ltd.

3 4 5 6 7 8 9 05 04 03

101 Facts About

TROPICAL FISH

Sarah Williams

Gareth Stevens Publishing
A WORLD ALMANAC EDUCATION GROUP COMPANY

2 Marine fish (left) live in salt water and are quite difficult to keep as pets. Most people have freshwater tropical fish.

1 Fish have been around for the last 400 million years. They are **aquatic vertebrates**, which means they are creatures that have a backbone and live in the water.

3 Altogether, there are more than 24,600 species, or kinds, of fish. Of these, only 8,000 are freshwater tropical fish.

4 Like people, fish have five senses — sight, smell, hearing, taste, and touch.

4

7 Scales are clear. They do not have any color. The bright colors of tropical fish come from the pigments, or colors, in the skin right under the scales.

5 Fish live underwater, but they still need oxygen. They breathe through gills on each side of their bodies. Gills are vents that filter oxygen out of the water.

8 A fish that is totally colorless or transparent (see-through) has no color in its skin. The Glass Catfish (below) is transparent.

6 The bodies of most tropical fish are covered with scales made of a hard, bony material. They protect the fish from injuries.

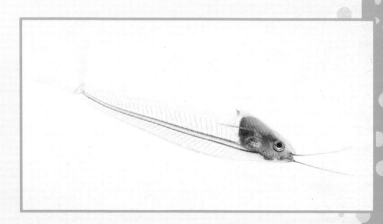

11 Some fish, such as the African Cichlid (below), are called **mouth brooders**. This means their eggs hatch inside the mouth of the mother fish! The fry live mainly inside her mouth until they are old enough to leave. They swim out to play and dart back in if they sense danger.

9 Tropical fish fall into two groups: fish that lay eggs (**egg layers**) and fish that give birth to live baby fish (**live bearers**).

10 Baby fish are called **fry**.

13 When its swim bladder is full, the fish can swim higher up in the water, closer to the surface. To swim close to the bottom, the fish empties its "balloon" and sinks.

12 Tropical fish have a special organ called a **swim bladder** inside their bodies. A swim bladder is like a balloon. When a fish breathes in, it can add air to its swim bladder. Because water is heavier than air, anything filled with air will float.

14 All fish have fins. The size and shape of its fins tell us a lot about the life and behavior of each fish.

15 Flat fish or thick, stocky fish, such as the Clown Loach (below), are designed to live on, or close to, the bottom.

16 Fish that are designed to live in open water have long, pointed fins and are **streamlined**, with long, smooth bodies that move easily through the water. Swordtail fish (above) are streamlined.

17 Fish that move more slowly tend to have rounded fins. The Oscar is one of these fish.

18 Each fin has a different way of helping the fish move through the water.

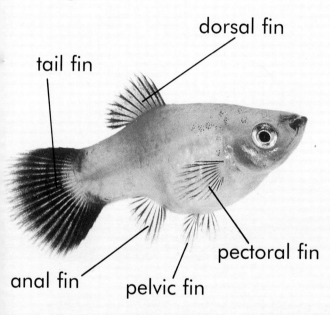

tail fin

dorsal fin

pectoral fin

anal fin

pelvic fin

19 The pectoral, or chest, fins are close to the fish's head, next to the gills. Pectoral fins help a fish turn, balance, and swim backward.

20 Pelvic fins come in pairs. They are like brakes that help a fish stop.

21 Dorsal and anal fins are found at the top and underside of the fish. These fins help keep the fish balanced.

22 The purpose of the tail fin is to push the fish forward. It may also help the fish turn and stop.

23 Fish need room to move around. Keep fish in a bowl that holds at least 1 gallon (4 liters).

up and down. A long tank gives them more room to move and is easier to clean.

24 Choose the largest tank you can afford and fit in your home. Glass tanks are better than acrylic (plastic) tanks because they are less likely to break.

25 Try to buy a long, rectangular tank instead of a tall one. Fish tend to swim backward and forward rather than

26 Tropical fish like warm water, but they need plenty of oxygen. The warmer the water is, the less oxygen it has. A long aquarium allows more air to be absorbed into the water, thus helping the fish breathe.

27 Most normal furniture is not strong enough to support a full aquarium. The best idea is to buy a specially made aquarium stand (right) for your tank.

28 An aquarium is very heavy when it is full. A 36-gallon (136-liter) tank will weigh about 300 pounds (136 kilograms) when it is full.

fish, and the Sun and heat may encourage the growth of **algae**, a type of fungus.

29 Do not put the tank in direct sunlight or next to a heater. The water can become too hot for the

30 Fish have excellent hearing. It is best not to put their tank too close to a television or stereo.

31 Every aquarium needs a cover, which is called the "hood."

32 A hood keeps unwanted things from getting inside the tank. It also keeps lively fish from jumping out of the aquarium when they are playing around!

33 The most important thing for keeping your fish healthy is good, clean water. Every aquarium should have a filter to remove poisons and pieces of dirt from the water.

34 Water can be acidic or alkaline. Acids and alkalies are chemicals that can burn, but water dilutes them. Usually, acids or alkalies in water are not strong enough to burn, but if your water is acidic or alkaline, it may hurt your fish.

37 Air stones are porous rocks that distribute the oxygen from the air pump. If cleaned well, they can also keep the water fresh.

35 Test your tank's acids and alkalies with a pH measuring kit, which you can buy at a pet store. If the water's pH is bad, ask the store for help.

38 Tropical fish like to swim in tropical temperatures. You will need a heater to keep the water warm and a thermometer to check the temperature.

36 Filters add oxygen to the water, but it is still a good idea to have an extra air pump for your tank.

13

39 Tanks should have a fluorescent light. This light is cool and has the same effect on fish and plants as natural daylight. Fish like up to 12 hours of daylight out of every 24 hours.

40 Some fish, such as Neon Tetra fish (below and left), reflect fluorescent light. If you look at one of these fish about an hour after you have turned out the lights, you will see that its bright stripe has faded and it is almost see-through.

41 You will need a thin layer of gravel for the bottom of your tank. Use only special aquarium gravel from your pet store. Natural gravel may pollute the water.

42 Pea-sized gravel is fine for most fish. Pet stores sell gravel in many different colors.

43 Coral is pretty, but it should be used for marine fish only — not for freshwater tropical fish.

44 You can add lots of decorations to your tank to brighten it up. Miniature caves and rocky cliffs will make your fish tank more like the fish's natural home.

45 Either artificial or live plants are fine for aquariums. Plants make the tank more interesting for you and your fish. Live plants can also be a source of food, but make sure the plants are healthy and all dead leaves are removed.

46 Many different backdrops are available for decorating your tank. A backdrop is a paper or plastic "scene" at the back of the aquarium.

47 After setting up the tank, wait 10 days before adding fish. This wait is necessary because the water must settle down, or "mature," before it is right for the fish.

48 While the water in your tank settles, choose what kind of fish you want. About 1,500 to 2,000 species of tropical fish are available to buy as pets.

49 Each species of tropical freshwater fish belongs to a particular group of fish. These groups are called **genera**.

50 The main groups kept by tropical fish owners are labyrinth fish, catfish, characiformes, cypriniforms, cyprinodonts, cichlids, and rainbow fish.

51 For a balanced fish community, keep certain species and families together.

52 Some fish form **schools**. That does not mean they have lessons! It means they swim around in groups. If you choose a species of fish that forms a school, be sure to buy at least five or six for the group.

53 Some fish, such as the Red Devil, can be aggressive and attack other fish. It is best not to keep those kinds. They might fight and upset the other fish.

54 When some fish argue over territory — the area they claim — they kiss! That is how these fish mark the edge of their personal space. Peaceful fish that "kiss" this way include Kissing Gouramis (above).

55 Fish grow throughout their whole lives. Make sure you know how big each species might get before you buy it. Otherwise, you could get a big surprise!

56 The Clown Loach (below) grows up to be about 14 inches (35 centimeters) long.

57 Make sure that all the fish you choose can live in the same range of temperature and in the same water conditions. Your pet store will advise you.

60 In an aquarium community, each fish will like living in its own part of the water. Some like to live near the top of the tank, some in the middle, and some near the bottom.

58 Make sure the store where you buy your fish is clean and takes good care of all its fish. Do not buy fish that have cuts or scratches.

61 **Top-dwelling** fish include the Platy, Guppy, Black Molly, Green Swordtail, White Cloud Mountain Minnow, Common Hatchetfish (below), and Siamese Fighting Fish.

59 A fish is not healthy if it has frayed fins, dull skin, or white spots that are not part of its normal coloring. Do not buy unhealthy fish.

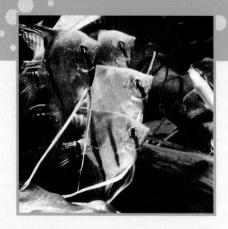

62 **Midwater** fish include the Rosy Barb, Red Rasbora, Neon Tetra, Angelfish (above), Blue Gourami, and Glass Catfish.

63 **Bottom-dwelling** fish include the Clown Loach, Red-tailed Shark, and Synodontis Catfish (below).

64 Fish for beginners to avoid include the Green Discus, the Oscar, the Red Devil, the Jack Dempsey, the Tinfoil Barb, the Sucking Loach, the Red Snakehead, the Piranha, and the Mudskipper.

65 After you have chosen your fish at the store, the sales person will probably give you the fish in a plastic bag filled with water.

66 Make sure that plenty of oxygen has been pumped into the top of the bag, and try to keep the bag as steady as possible on the trip home.

68 Once the temperature of the water in the bag is the same as that of the water in the tank, add a handful of water from the tank to the bag. Then let the bag float for another 15 minutes.

67 Do not pour the fish into your aquarium right away. Instead, let the full plastic bag float in the tank for 15 minutes (above). This allows the fish to get used to the temperature of the water in the tank.

69 Now add the fish to the tank by simply turning the bag upside down – gently!

21

70 When you choose your fish, make sure you know what foods they eat. Some fish are **carnivores** and eat only meat, some are **herbivores** and eat only plants, and some are **omnivores** and will eat both plants and meat.

71 When you first set up your aquarium, try to choose omnivores. They eat many kinds of food and are much easier to feed.

72 The shape and position of a fish's mouth can give you clues about what that fish eats.

73 Fish with upturned mouths (above) usually eat insects that live on the surface of the water.

74 Fish with forward-pointing mouths (below) usually live and feed in midwater.

22

75 Fish with down-turned mouths (right) usually eat creatures that live at the bottom in the sand, soil, or plants.

76 Some fish, like the Suckermouth catfish (below), have huge, sucker-like lips. These lips allow the fish to attach itself to a surface and browse for food.

77 Other fish have **barbels** sticking out from their lips (above). Barbels resemble whiskers. They let the fish "feel" the water and sense any food that might be in it.

78 Some fish have teeth. The teeth of fish are made of dentine and are similar to human teeth.

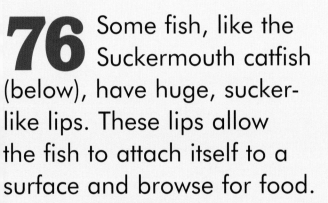

79 The most famous pointy-toothed fish is probably the Piranha (above). This fish is a fierce carnivore and is best left to the experts.

80 Unlike human teeth, fish teeth are always growing and being replaced. It does not matter if a fish's teeth are broken. New teeth will grow in.

81 Why fish have teeth is a mystery. Most fish do not seem to chew their food. In fact, they often swallow the food whole.

82 The main part of your fish's diet should be dried fish food (below). It contains all the things your fish need to stay healthy. Two flakes for each fish is about the right amount for an average tank.

83 Dried food comes in flakes, pellets, or tablets. Most fish will be fine with flakes, but you should give pellets to larger fish or fish that live at the bottom of the tank.

84 Give your fish different foods several times a week. They can get bored with flakes or pellets all the time. The fish below are feeding on a tablet food.

85 Your fish can eat many household foods. Carnivorous fish can eat raw fish, raw meat, egg yolk, and chicken. Cooked potatoes, cauliflower, beans, broccoli, peas, uncooked spinach, and lettuce (below) are good for herbivores.

food products from a good pet store. Some live foods can carry diseases and make your fish sick.

86 If you give your fish any household food, you must chop it up quite small, so it is the same size as a food pellet. Drop in only two to three lumps of food for each fish.

88 Feed your fish over a five-minute period. Offer a little at a time. Wait for the fish to eat it all before you add more. Stop after five minutes.

87 Fish also like live food. Brine shrimp, earthworms, tubifex worms, whiteworms, and blood-worms can all be fed to your fish. You should always buy

89 Always feed your fish at the same time of day and in the same area of the tank.

90 Fish are greedy and will eat as much as you give them. Most have small stomachs, however. Did you know that a fish's stomach is about the same size as its eye? Even if your fish beg, never overfeed them because that can make them very sick.

91 If you go away on vacation, you can leave your fish without food for up to three days. If you will be gone longer than that, however, you should either get someone to come in and feed them or use an automatic food dispenser, which feeds your fish for you.

92 Feeding is not the only chore you will need to do. You must check different parts of your tank every day, week, month, and year.

93 Each day, you will need to feed the fish, turn the lights on and off, and check the filters, temperature, and air pump.

94 About once each week, change some of the water (about one-fifth of the water, or 20 percent), vacuum the gravel, feed and trim the plants, clean the inside of the tank glass with an algae cleaning pad, and check all the filter parts.

95 You may empty the tank once a year. Save most of the water to use again. Change the filter parts, wash everything, and rinse off all the soap. Check the water temperature before you put the fish back.

96 Fish do not like sudden changes of temperature. Sudden changes can make them very sick and may even kill them.

97 Signs of illness include white or fuzzy spots, rapid breathing, twitching, swimming in odd patterns, and lack of motion.

98 One of the first signs of a sick fish is its lack of interest in food.

99 Sometimes you might have to **quarantine** a fish, or keep it away from the other fish, in a separate tank called a hospital tank.

100 If your fish becomes sick, ask your **veterinarian** or pet store for help and advice.

101 If you take good care of your tropical fish, they should stay healthy, look great in your home, and give you a fascinating hobby.

Glossary

algae: a fungus that grows inside an aquarium. Too much algae in a tank can harm the fish.

aquatic vertebrates: creatures that have a backbone and live in water.

barbels: whiskerlike feelers.

bottom-dwelling: living at the bottom of the tank.

carnivores: animals that eat meat.

egg layers: fish that lay eggs.

fry: baby fish.

genera: a group that includes various species.

herbivores: animals that eat only plants.

live bearers: fish that give birth to live babies.

midwater: living in the middle depth of the aquarium's water.

mouth brooders: fish that carry their babies in their mouths.

omnivores: animals that eat both plants and meat.

quarantine: to keep a sick animal away from the others so its illness cannot spread.

schools: groups of fish that swim around together.

streamlined: long and smooth, allowing water or air to move easily over the body.

swim bladder: an organ inside some fish's bodies that allows fish to swim higher or lower, depending on how much air is in it.

top-dwelling: living in the upper part of the aquarium's water.

veterinarian: a doctor who treats animals.

More Books to Read

All About Tropical Fishkeeping
Steve Windsor
(Barron's Educational)

ASPCA Pet Care Guides for Kids:
Fish Mark Evans and Roger A.
Caras (DK Publishing)

Fish (All about Pets series)
Helen Frost (Pebble Books)

Me and My Pet Fish
Christine Morley and Carole
Orbell (Two-Can)

Web Sites

All About Fish
www.geocities.com/mpreseau1/

AquariumFish.net
www.aquariumfish.net

Fins: Fish Information Service
www.actwin.com/fish/index.php

Fish Frequently Asked Questions
www.wh.whoi.edu/faq/

To find additional web sites, use a reliable search engine, such as www.yahooligans.com, with one or more of the following keywords: **aquariums, fishkeeping, tropical fish, tropical fish species**.

Index